Leading Lady

PRINCESS CAROLINE OF MONACO

By: Jill C. Wheeler

Published by Abdo & Daughters, 6535 Cecilia Circle, Edina, Minnesota 55439.

Library bound edition distributed by Rockbottom Books, Pentagon Tower, P.O. Box 36036, Minneapolis, Minnesota 55435.

Printed in the United States.

Cover Photo: Retna LTD
Inside Photos: UPI Bettmann 4,6,7,9,11,16,19,24,30 &32
                Archive Photos 14,22,26 & 28

Edited by Rosemary Wallner

LIBRARY OF CONGRESS CATALOGING-IN-PUBLICATION DATA
Wheeler, Jill C., 1964-
    Princess Caroline / written by Jill C. Wheeler.
       p. cm. — (Leading Ladies)
    Summary: A look at the public and private life of Monaco's First Lady.
    ISBN 1-56239-117-8
    1. Caroline, Princess of Monaco, 1957- -- Juvenile literature. 2. Monaco -- Princess and princesses -- Biography -- Juvenile literature. [1. Caroline, Princess of Monaco, 1957- . 2. Princesses.] I. Title. II. Series.
DC943.C37W44 1992   944.9'49--dc20   92-16676
                                              [B]

International Standard	Library of Congress
Book Number:	Catalog Card Number:
1-56239-117-8	92-16676

TABLE OF CONTENTS

Princess Caroline's first birthday, with her mother Princess Grace of Monaco.

HER ROYAL HIGHNESS

Few people have spent their lives in the public spotlight as much as Princess Caroline of Monaco. The Princess is the oldest daughter of Monaco's reigning Prince Ranier III (pronounced Ray-nay) and his wife, the late actress Grace Kelly.

A twenty-one-gun salute announced Princess Caroline Louise Marguerite's arrival on January 23, 1957. Since then, photographers and reporters have followed her nearly everywhere she goes. Her loves, activities and opinions have made news around the world.

Monaco is one of the few countries in the world that still have royal heads of state. The tiny country is the size of New York City's Central Park. It is 435 miles south-southeast of Paris between the French Alps and the beautiful Riviera coastline. Millions of people visit the country every year to enjoy the beautiful weather and many activities there.

Monaco's reigning Grimaldi family is another reason why the country is so famous. A member of the Grimaldi family has ruled Monaco since the thirteenth century. It is no surprise the world was all eyes and ears when Caroline's father, Prince Ranier, took a bride in 1956.

Grimaldi (Rainier of Grimaut), early 14th century French Admiral.

SCENES FROM A FAIRY TALE

Many thought Prince Ranier III of Monaco was the world's most eligible bachelor. He met American movie star Grace Kelly in 1955. Rumors quickly spread about Kelly and the dashing prince. The two married in a fairy tale wedding on April 19, 1956.

Prince Rainier III and Grace Kelly as they are joined in wedlock, April 19, 1956.

Many Monaco residents, called Monégasques, had doubts about their new Princess. She was the daughter of a bricklayer from Philadelphia. Some thought the Prince should have married a woman of royal blood.

Princess Grace quickly won over the residents of Monaco with her warmth and charm. She became even more popular with the birth of baby Caroline. Now Monaco had a royal heir. Prince Ranier declared a national holiday on the birth day of his first child.

Caroline was officially named heiress to the throne of Monaco when she was two days old. She would remain heiress until she had a brother. She also had the distinction of having both Monaco and American citizenship.

Almost immediately everyone wanted to see a picture of Caroline. Prince Ranier had photographers bid for the right to photograph his new daughter.

He donated the money he raised to the Monaco Red Cross. The right to photograph the baby went to a friend of Princess Grace. The pictures appeared in *Look* and later *Life* magazines.

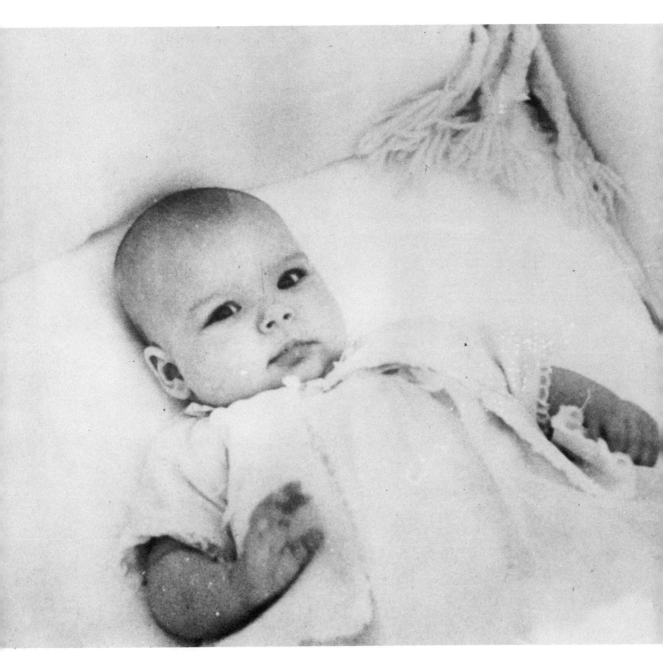

5-month-old Princess Caroline of Monaco lying in her cradle.

Princess Caroline's progress made headlines through-out the world. People were curious to know what the baby was doing as she grew. Her mother gave fre-quent reports to the press to answer their questions.

"I think she looks more and more like the Prince," Princess Grace said. Her daughter was five-and-a-half weeks old then. "She has dark blue eyes like Ranier, much darker than mine, and his broad forehead. She has a lovely complexion, absolutely without blemish, and light brown hair."

That report was just the beginning. As she grew, cam-eras and eager reporters often hounded Princess Caroline. The arrival of a brother, Prince Albert Alexandre Louis in 1958, and a sister, Princess Stephanie Marie Elisabeth, in 1965, barely changed things. As the first child of a fairy tale marriage, she would always be of interest in the public eye.

L-R, Princess Caroline, 9, Prince Albert, 8, and Princess Stephanie, 19 months, all sitting with their mother, Princess Grace.

GROWING UP A PRINCESS

Princess Caroline had many of the same experiences as other little girls – only on a much larger scale. Four bishops and fifteen priests conducted her christening. Her bedroom was a suite of rooms in the 180-room castle. It had two bedrooms, a playroom and a kitchen with its own refrigerator. She had more than one hundred stuffed toys, plus both a nurse and a nanny. The baby princess couldn't read, yet she received hundreds of fan letters each week.

Princess Grace worried that her children might be spoiled by growing up as royalty. She ordered they be disciplined when necessary. She limited the amount of television they could watch. She also encouraged them to take part in sports. Princess Caroline excelled at swimming. She also water skied, snow skied, sailed, took horseback riding lessons and played tennis. Sometimes she behaved like a bossy older sister, too.

Being royal, Caroline also had some official duties. Once she was on a trip to Ireland with her father. She saw people gathering around the British leader Winston Churchill and asked her nanny, "Is he more important than my daddy?"

"I was the most horrible child," Caroline said many years later. "I never wanted to sit on anybody's lap, including my mother's. She was a very frustrated young mother when she had me. I was always squirming out of people's arms."

The Grimaldi children also frequently visited the United States. They visited their mother's family in Philadelphia. Caroline went to Disneyland when she was ten years old. When she was nineteen, the family visited Wyoming and New Mexico.

In between, there were ballet and music lessons, Girl Scouts, picnics and school plays. Many people wondered if Caroline would follow in her mother's footsteps and pursue acting. Caroline acted in two plays as a child but said she was not interested in it as a career. "Acting – absolutely never," she said. "Then I'd be compared to my mom."

Caroline had a private tutor until she was seven years old. After that, she attended private Catholic schools – along with her bodyguard. Caroline was sent to a Catholic boarding school in England when she was fourteen. She was considered a good scholar and could speak French, English, German and Spanish.

*Princess Caroline was very active as a child, she participated
in plays and took ballet.*

At age eighteen, she enrolled in the Institut d'Etudes Politiques in Paris. There, Caroline took classes in economics, finance, international relations and constitutional law. Some reporters claimed she spent more time at the Paris nightclubs than she did in classes. When exam time came, she did not pass and had to leave the school.

A REBELLIOUS ROYAL

Princess Caroline's life had been very sheltered. By the time she turned eighteen, she was ready for a little freedom and adventure. "I was raised with a sense of duty, obedience and ... guilt," she said many years later. "What I had to do always came before what I wanted to do."

Caroline showed her new independence in many ways. She and sister Stephanie had always loved fashion. They often wore clothing from famous designers. They also enjoyed wearing jeans – something their father did not like. He forbade his wife to wear pants at all. Caroline was especially glad to be rid of the uniforms she had to wear at her school.

*Princess Caroline (L) and Stephanie make a dazzling entrance at the
Monte Carlo Sporting Club.*

The Grimaldi sisters often stayed out until dawn going to parties and dances. They were popular and beautiful. They also were eager to get away from the strictness of their royal lives. As Caroline later wrote in an article, "Monaco is a small town and everybody knows everybody else. By the time we reached our teen years we longed for some kind of action. It was not only boring. We were too protected. When would we be allowed to escape? Where was the adventure we deserved?"

Caroline found the freedom she wanted in Paris. There, she attended parties and danced with dashing young men. Her dates included a songwriter, an actor and a rich British playboy. None of the relationships lasted long, however. Then she met a man who was to change the course of her life.

THE PRINCESS MEETS A PLAYBOY

In the summer of 1976, Princess Caroline met Phillipe Junot at a party in Paris. Junot caught her attention because he did not treat her like royalty. Junot was seventeen years older than Caroline and from a wealthy French family. No one was certain what he did for a living – if he did anything at all.

Princess Caroline enjoyed spending time with the fun-loving Junot. He led the kind of life she had always wanted but never had. She refused to enroll at Princeton University in the United States as her parents wanted her to. Instead, she took classes at the Sorbonne in Paris so she could be with Junot.

In early 1977, Junot asked Caroline to marry him. She accepted, but she still needed her parents' permission. That was not easy to get.

Ranier and Grace had hoped for a better match for their oldest daughter. They wanted someone of royal blood, or at least someone from an upper-class family. Yet they did not want to protest too loudly against Junot. They were afraid Caroline would stop talking to them if they did. Instead, they asked Caroline to wait to get married until she was older.

Caroline agreed to her parents' plan, but she continued to see Junot. After several more months, her parents said she and Junot could get married in a year. Nine months later, Caroline asked permission to get married and her father refused. Caroline was very angry and threatened to move in with Junot. Ranier knew such a move would upset the people of Monaco. He changed his mind and allowed the marriage.

To be married: Princess Caroline and her fiance, Phillipe Junot.

Princess Grace still was not happy about her daughter's marriage. However, she decided to give her a beautiful wedding. The wedding, on June 29, 1978, was a major event. Many kings and queens, as well as Hollywood movie stars, attended. Caroline's sister refused to attend. She said it was because she did not like Junot.

The newlyweds took off for a three-week honeymoon in Tahiti. The honeymoon stretched into two years as the couple visited the U.S., Greece, the West Indies and Scotland. Finally, they settled in an apartment in Paris. They continued to visit the Paris night spots and Junot remained a popular party-goer.

Caroline also took time out to help with charities. She worked with UNICEF and started a telephone hotline to help teenagers facing problems in their lives. She finished a degree in child psychology from the Sorbonne. Many people thought she had ended her rebellious years.

HEARTBREAK TIMES TWO

Less than two years after her wedding, Caroline found out Junot had been with other women. Photographers even had pictures of him with other women while he was on business trips. Caroline had to admit she had made a mistake. By June 1980 she decided to end the marriage. The couple received a divorce on October 9, 1980.

After the divorce, Caroline retreated to her parents' home in Monaco. She dealt with her broken heart in privacy and with help from her family. "Some people need friends more than others," she told a friend later. "I have friends, but I don't have a best friend. I have never felt the need to confide in anybody. I've always felt that when I had a problem I could find the solution within myself." Meanwhile, Junot continued to travel the world, still a playboy.

Later Caroline admitted her marriage had been a mistake. "I wouldn't have married so young the first time," she told an interviewer in 1985. "I wanted to get away from home, so it seemed a rather classical way of doing it. I wasn't allowed to go live on my own. I had to live at home with my parents, so I had to find the next best way of convincing them."

Less than two years after her divorce, tragedy again struck Princess Caroline's life. Princess Grace died after her car crashed near the family's country home. Suddenly Princess Caroline faced life without her mother. She also had to take over as the First Lady of Monaco and help her grief-stricken father.

Princess Grace dies in a tragic car accident: At the funeral; Prince Albert, Prince Rainier and Princess Caroline.

Princess Caroline showed strength and courage in the months following her mother's death. She made Grace's funeral arrangements and consoled her father. She took up writing and published articles in two newspapers. She filled in for her mother at social functions, including a luncheon with French President Francois Mitterrand. She attended a benefit in the United States at which Grace had been scheduled to speak.

A SECOND CHANCE AT LOVE

Eventually Caroline began to date again. Her boyfriends included tennis star Guillermo Vilas and Robertino Rosellini, the son of Ingrid Bergman and director Roberto Rosellini. Rosellini was a special comfort to the Princess after her mother's death. Rumors of marriage between the two circulated, but the relationship ended in the summer of 1983. At one point, Caroline wrote in her journal, "I do not think I am the ideal woman for a man – with my tormented past, my uncertain present and perhaps my melancholy future."

Caroline's thoughts changed when she began spending time with Stefano Casiraghi in the summer of 1983. Casiraghi was just twenty-three years old when he began seeing Caroline, then twenty-eight years old.

Princess Caroline and husband Stefano Casiraghi.

Prince Ranier again became concerned that young Casiraghi might not be a sound choice for his daughter. Casiraghi had a reputation as a hardworking businessman and a big spender.

Ranier changed his mind after getting to know the young man. In December, the Prince announced that his daughter had married the handsome blond Italian. Unlike her first marriage, she and Casiraghi tied the knot in a quiet civil ceremony with only family and friends in attendance.

PRINCESS MOM

The following year Princess Caroline and Casiraghi had their first child, son Andrea. Andrea received a sister Charlotte, in August 1986 and a brother, Pierre, in September 1987. The three children, plus her duties as Monaco's First Lady, made Princess Caroline's life very busy.

Caroline, like her mother, was determined her children would have as normal a life as possible. She enjoyed bathing and dressing her children, telling them bedtime stories and cooking the family's meals. She also had a staff of two nannies, a secretary, a maid and a security guard to help.

"I hope nobody thinks that I leave the raising of my children to others," she said. "I spend enormous amounts of time with them."

Princess Caroline, with her husband and their three children; in her father's lap is daughter Charlotte, baby son Pierre and first son Andrea.

Caroline's role as First Lady was much like a job. She had an office, where she worked from 10:30 a.m. to 5:00 p.m. each weekday. Here she helped out with many of the charities in her small country and advanced the the cultural projects founded by her mother. As the First Lady, she was honorary head of such organizations as the Garden Club, the Girl Guides and the Ladies Needle and Thread Society. She also served as president of the Princess Grace Foundation, which raises money to help artists around the globe.

A special project of Princess Grace had been to bring a ballet company to Monaco. Caroline, who had studied ballet for ten years, put in many hours of work to see her mother's wishes fulfilled. She was especially happy in December 1985 when the Ballets de Monte Carlo put on its first performance.

Caroline's work for Monaco was praised by many, but Caroline wanted mostly to be a wife and mother. "It wouldn't bother me at all if I weren't Princess Caroline of Monaco," she said once. "I prefer to be at home with my husband and children than attacked by photographers. I'm just the sister of the future Prince, and my children come first. I work my schedule around them."

TRAGEDY STRIKES AGAIN

Casiraghi also led a busy life. In addition to his business, he loved dangerous sports. His favorites were powerboat racing and car racing. "You must not be scared of going too fast," Casiraghi said. Caroline often brought the children to watch their father race. She also worried about his safety.

Princess Caroline, with husband, Casiraghi, enjoying one of their favorite pastimes, powerboatracing.

Once Casiraghi was driving in a cross-country auto race from France to Morocco. His car overturned in the Moroccan Desert. He was rescued by a group of photographers who had been following him. Another time she saw Casiraghi's boat disappear in a cloud of smoke during a race. Luckily, he was not hurt.

That luck came to an end on October 3, 1990. Casiraghi, the world off-shore powerboat champion, was racing off the coast of Monaco. His boat was traveling ninety-three miles per hour when it flew into the air and flipped upside down. Casiraghi died instantly, leaving a thirty-three-year-old widow with three children.

BRAVE FACE FORWARD

The time since her husband's death has been very difficult for Princess Caroline. She went into mourning immediately after Casiraghi's death. Each day, she visited his tomb dressed all in black. She did not appear in public until May 1991. When she did appear, many people commented on how she looked. She had cut her hair short and had lost weight. Some people said she looked pale and strained.

Tragedy strikes again in Princess Caroline's life; mourning the death of her husband.

As with her divorce and her mother's death, Caroline has turned to her family for support. She and her children spend many hours together in the French country home she shared with Casiraghi. She also continues working with her father as Monaco's First Lady. She will have that job until her brother, Albert, marries.

"First Lady. It's a big word, as if there were a hierarchy of ladies," she said. "I work for my country as everyone else here works. If I can do something in an area I know a bit about, that's very well. In the end it's a job like any other."

Princess Caroline's charm and beauty have made her Monaco's most famous ambassador. Her work for the country also has carried her through many difficult times and promises to do so again.

Whatever the future may bring, those who know Caroline say she will recover from the tragedies that have haunted her life. A former spokeswoman for the royal family summed it up. "Princess Caroline has been self-assured and independent since she was born," the woman said. "It will take her some time to rebound from this tragedy. But rebound she will."

Princess Caroline's charm and beauty have made her Monaco's most famous ambassador.